DATE DUE

DATE DUE	
JAN 0 4 2008	
JAN 1 4 2008	
FEB 0 8 2008	
FEB 0 8 2008	
JUN 1 5 2011	
OCT 2 9 2013	

DEMCO, INC. 38-2931

I USE MATH

I USE MATH AT THE DOCTOR'S

by Joanne Mattern
Reading consultant: Susan Nations, M.Ed., author/literacy coach/consultant

WR WEEKLY READER
EARLY LEARNING LIBRARY

Please visit our web site at: www.earlyliteracy.cc
For a free color catalog describing Weekly Reader® Early Learning Library's list
of high-quality books, call 1-877-445-5824 (USA) or 1-800-387-3178 (Canada).
Weekly Reader® Early Learning Library's fax: (414) 336-0164.

Library of Congress Cataloging-in-Publication Data available upon request from publisher.
Fax (414) 336-0157 for the attention of the Publishing Records Department.

ISBN 0-8368-4854-3 (lib. bdg.)
ISBN 0-8368-4861-6 (softcover)

This edition first published in 2006 by
Weekly Reader® Early Learning Library
A Member of the WRC Media Family of Companies
330 West Olive Street, Suite 100
Milwaukee, WI 53212 USA

Managing editor: Valerie J. Weber
Art direction: Tammy West
Cover design and page layout: Dave Kowalski
Photo research: Diane Laska-Swanke
Photographer: Gregg Andersen

Printed in the United States of America

1 2 3 4 5 6 7 8 9 09 08 07 06 05

Note to Educators and Parents

Reading is such an exciting adventure for young children! They are beginning to integrate their oral language skills with written language. To encourage children along the path to early literacy, books must be colorful, engaging, and interesting; they should invite the young reader to explore both the print and the pictures.

I Use Math is a new series designed to help children read about using math in their everyday lives. In each book, young readers will explore a different activity and solve math problems along the way.

Each book is specially designed to support the young reader in the reading process. The familiar topics are appealing to young children and invite them to read — and reread — again and again. The full-color photographs and enhanced text further support the student during the reading process.

In addition to serving as wonderful picture books in schools, libraries, homes, and other places where children learn to love reading, these books are specifically intended to be read within an instructional guided reading group. This small group setting allows beginning readers to work with a fluent adult model as they make meaning from the text. After children develop fluency with the text and content, the book can be read independently. Children and adults alike will find these books supportive, engaging, and fun!

— Susan Nations, M.Ed., author, literacy coach, and consultant in literacy development

Today, I am going to the doctor for a checkup. There are many people in the waiting room.

How many people are in the waiting room?

4

Our appointment is at 1:00. Mom reads a book to me while we wait.

What time is it now? How long do I have to wait?

It is our turn! The
nurse measures my
height. She says I
am getting tall!

How tall am I?

8

Mom says there are twelve inches in a foot.

How many inches are there in two feet?

10

PALOS PARK LIBRARY
PALOS PARK, IL 60464

11

Next, the nurse asks me to stand on a scale. The scale shows how many pounds I weigh.

How much do I weigh?

The nurse shows me my chart. I weigh four pounds more than I did last year.

How much did I weigh last year?

The doctor takes my temperature. He also looks in my eyes, ears, and mouth.

How many instruments is the doctor using to check on me?

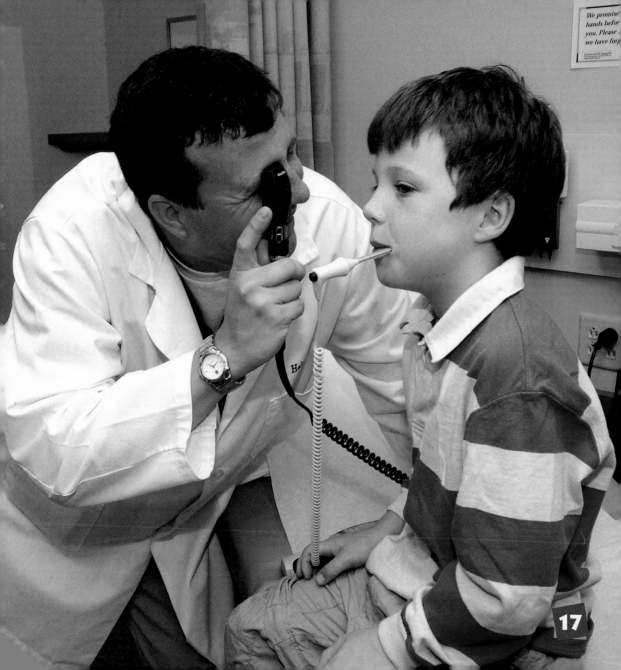

The doctor listens to my heart with a stethoscope. Then, I listen, too. My heart beats once every second.

There are sixty seconds in one minute. How many times does my heart beat in one minute?

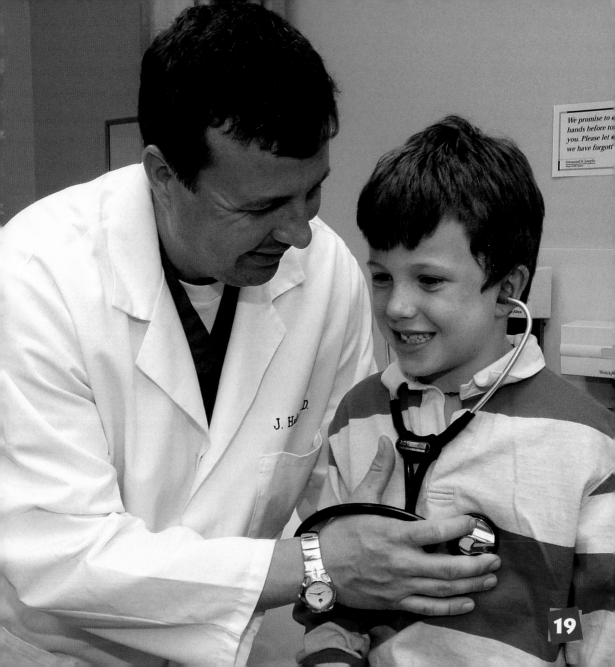

My checkup is done! I am healthy. The doctor lets me pick a sticker. I pick the blue one. I like going to the doctor's!

Which number sticker do I pick?
Hint: Start counting at the top of the stickers.

Glossary

appointment — a time to meet someone

checkup — an exam by a doctor to make sure you are not sick

height — how tall you are

instruments — tools to find something out

stethoscope — an instrument used to listen to your heartbeat

temperature — a measurement used to see if you have a fever

weigh — how heavy someone is

Answers

Page 4 – 8

Page 6 – 12:30, one-half hour

Page 8 – 49 inches

Page 10 – 24

Page 12 – 59 pounds

Page 14 – 55 pounds

Page 16 – 2

Page 18 – 60 times

Page 20 – 3

For More Information

Books

Counting: Follow That Fish! Math Monsters (series).
  John Burstein (Weekly Reader® Learning Library)
Doctor. People in My Community (series).
  Jacqueline Laks Gorman
  (Weekly Reader® Learning Library)
Going to the Doctor. Melinda Beth Radabaugh
  (Heinemann Library)
How Tall, How Short, How Far Away. David Adler
  (Holiday House)

Websites

A+ Math
www.aplusmath.com/games/index.html
Math games to practice your skills

Index

About the Author

Joanne Mattern is the author of more than 130 books for children. Her favorite subjects are animals, history, sports, and biography. Joanne lives in New York State with her husband, three young daughters, and three crazy cats.